Going Shopping

By Diane Church
Photographs by Chris Fairclough

W
FRANKLIN WATTS
NEW YORK·LONDON·SYDNEY

Moya and Sara are best friends. They both love clothes and today they are going shopping. Sara is physically disabled so she uses her wheelchair to go around the shops.

Sara has Muscular Dystrophy which makes her muscles weak. She finds it difficult to stand or walk.

First thing in the morning, Sara's mum helps to put splints on to Sara's legs. "Hurry up, mum," Sara tells her. "Moya's waiting downstairs for me!"

"I'm nearly ready," Sara calls out to her friend.

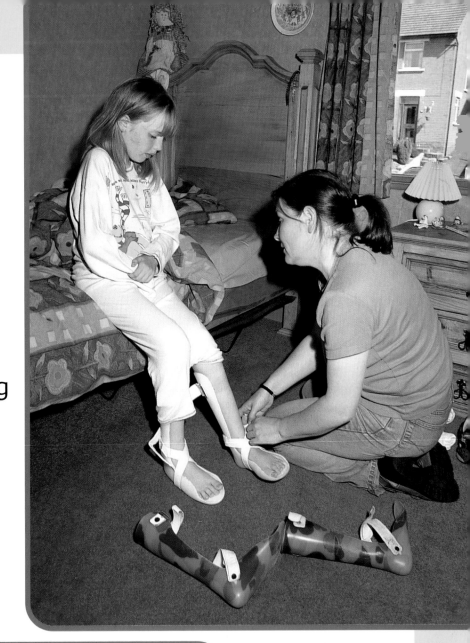

Sara wears splints to support her legs. She doesn't have enough strength to pull herself out of bed or walk downstairs so her mum helps her.

"Shall we get something to eat first?" Moya asks as she helps Sara into her wheelchair. "Good idea, I'm starving!" Sara replies.

"See you later," Sara's dad tells them. "I'll drive you all to the shops when you get back."

Sara and Moya count the number of difficulties they come across in the street. They try to find one for each letter of the alphabet.
"Animals, bins, cars," says Moya.
"Don't forget 'd' for dog's mess!" giggles Sara.

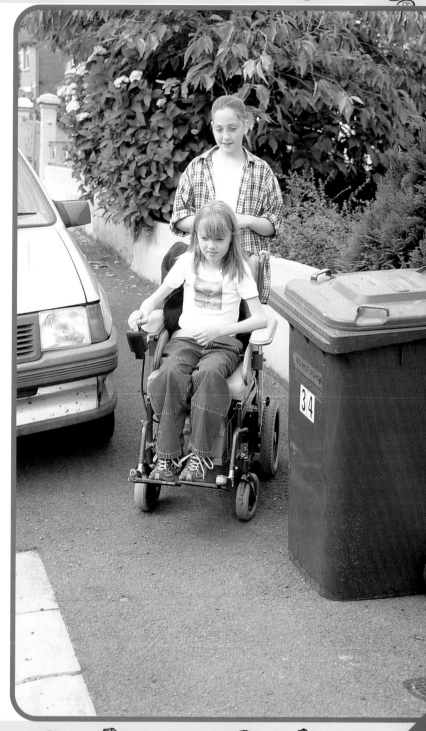

Sara only uses her wheelchair when she goes out. It takes up too much room to use indoors.

"Let's go to the cafe in the park," suggests Moya.

When they get there, Moya opens the door. "There's a step," Sara says. "Can you help me to get in?"

Automatic doors and ramps make it easy for people who use wheelchairs to get in and out of buildings.

Moya makes space for Sara to move her wheelchair to the table. "Shall we share some chips?" Moya asks.

The girls chat about what they want to buy. "I really want a new t-shirt for my holiday," Sara says.

When the girls have eaten they make their way home. They stop to feed some pigeons. "Let's go before the battery on my wheelchair runs out," says Sara.

Sara prefers her electric wheelchair, but the battery only lasts for 3 or 4 hours before it runs out.

At home the girls get changed and ready to go to the shopping mall. "I'll put in the manual wheelchair," Sara's dad thinks as he loads the car.

A manual wheelchair is operated by the person using it or by someone pushing it.

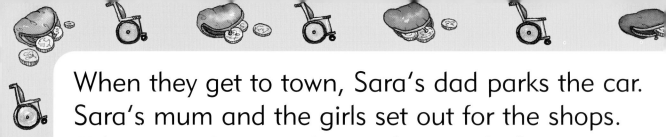

When they get to town, Sara's dad parks the car. Sara's mum and the girls set out for the shops. "I hope you've got plenty of money!" Sara says to her mum.

This is a safe but difficult place to cross the road as the kerb is high. It is best to use a crossing or traffic lights.

Sara sees a top she likes in a shop window. They go inside. "Oh no, the children's department is upstairs and there's no lift," Sara says.

They leave the wheelchair and Sara's mum carries her upstairs.

Shops in some buildings only have stairs. There are often lifts in newer buildings.

Sara and Moya look at the clothes.
"Look at this!" says Moya.
"It really suits you!"

"Wouldn't you love a hat like this?" Sara giggles. She tries on a fake fur scarf, too. They take it in turns to find funny things to wear.

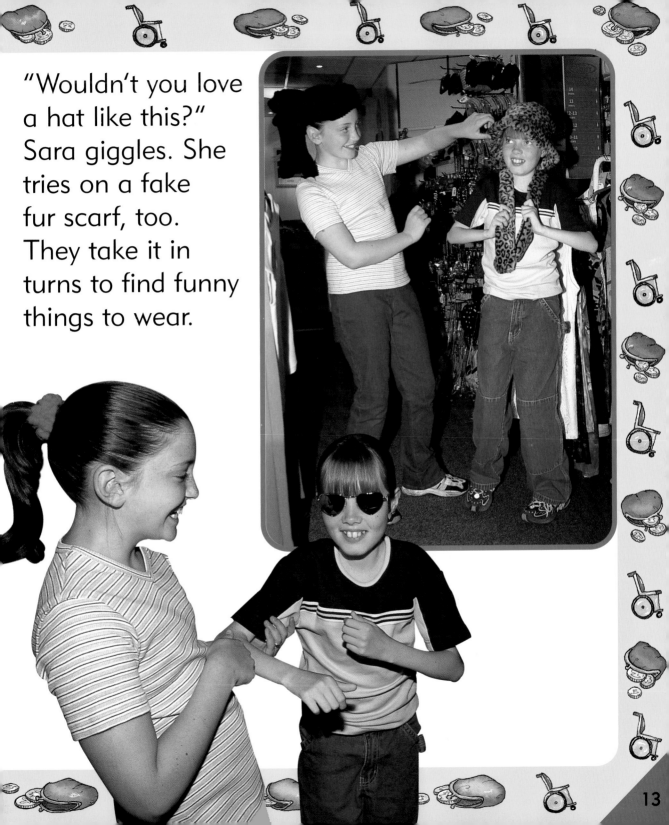

"Come on, let's look at something we want to buy," says Moya.

"Do you like this t-shirt?" Sara asks. They decide on the blue top.

Next they go to the shopping mall. They use the lift to reach the second floor. In the newsagents, the girls look at their favourite magazines. "Moya, can you pass me that one?" Sara asks.

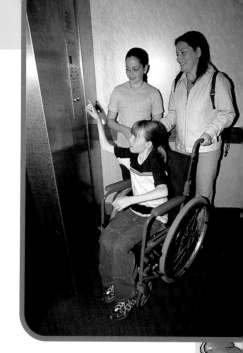

Many items in shops are out of reach for a person who is sitting in a wheelchair.

Now it's time to go home. "I'm going down on the escalator," Moya says.

"See you at the bottom!" Sara tells her.

It is not safe for people in wheelchairs to use an escalator. Sara and her mum use the lift again.

To get home they are catching a train.
They arrive early at the station so the guard
has time to get a ramp for the wheelchair.
"Thank you for your help," Sara says.

A ramp allows Sara to get on and off the train in her wheelchair.

On the train, Sara and Moya talk about the things they have bought.
"I'm really pleased with my t-shirt," says Sara.
"I'm exhausted!" says Moya.

On the train there is an area for Sara and her wheelchair. There's a seat for Moya, too.

When the girls get home, Sara has an idea.
"Let's go rollerblading! You can hold onto
my electric wheelchair and we'll go really fast!"
she says to her friend.
"Brilliant! This beats shopping any day!"
laughs Moya.

Facts about people with physical disabilities

★ When a part of someone's body does not work as expected, it is called a physical disability.

★ There are many different physical disabilities. Sara's body has been weakened by Muscular Dystrophy. This makes it hard for Sara to support her weight. Another physically disabled person may not be able to see or may not be able to use both their arms or legs.

★ Some people are born physically disabled. Some conditions, such as Muscular Dystrophy, start at different ages and develop further as you grow older. Some people are disabled because they have had an accident.

★ It is easy to think people with physical disabilities need a lot of help. Remember, people who are physically disabled are able to do lots of things but in a different way.

Glossary

muscular dystrophy   a condition that makes your muscles weak, so it becomes hard to support your body.

physically disabled   when a part of your body is damaged and you are unable to do some activities.

ramps   when the floor is sloped. People who cannot climb steps need a ramp to get into a building or onto a train. Lifts and doors that open automatically also make it easier for people who use wheelchairs to get around.

wheelchair   some wheelchairs are electric and run on a battery. Others are manual and the person using it has to turn the wheels themselves or get someone to push them.

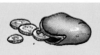

Try to be helpful

★ **1.** Offer to hold doors open to allow the person using a wheelchair to enter a building.

★ **2.** If you see a person with physical disabilities who looks as though they may need your help, ask them. Listen to their answer. People who are physically disabled can often manage on their own.

★ **3.** Ask your family and friends not to park their cars, leave bicycles or put wheelie bins on the pavement. It makes it hard for people to pass by.

★ **4.** It is important to include people who are physically disabled in your everyday life.

★ **5.** Remember, people with physical disabilities may have the same interests and hobbies as you. Why don't you do them together?

Further information and addresses

Muscular Dystrophy Campaign
7-11 Prescott Place
London
SW4 6BS
info@muscular-dystrophy.org
www.muscular-dystrophy.org

Muscular Dystrophy Association
Royal South Sydney Health
Complex
Joynton Avenue
Zetland
N.S.W. 2017, Australia
www.mda.org.au

RADAR – The Royal Association for
Disability and Rehabilitation
12 City Forum
250 City Road
London
EC1V 8AF
Minicom 0207 250 4119
radar@radar.org.uk
www.radar.org.uk

REACH National Advice Centre
for Children with Reading Difficulties
California Country Park
Nine Mile Ride,
Finchampstead, RG40 4HT
www.reach-reading.demon.co.uk

Index

© 2000 Franklin Watts

Franklin Watts
96 Leonard Street
London
EC2A 4XD

Franklin Watts Australia
14 Mars Road
Lane Cove
NSW 2066

ISBN: 0 7496 3671 8

Dewey Decimal Classification
Number: 362.4

10 9 8 7 6 5 4 3 2 1

A CIP catalogue record for
this book is available from the
British Library.

Printed in Malaysia

Consultants: Paula Keaveney,
The Muscular Dystrophy Campaign;
Beverley Mathias, REACH.
Editor: Samantha Armstrong
Designer: Louise Snowdon
Photographer: Chris Fairclough
Illustrator: Eliz Hüseyin

With thanks to: Sara Tipping and Moya Kelly
and their families.